JAMES KRENOV WORKER IN WOOD

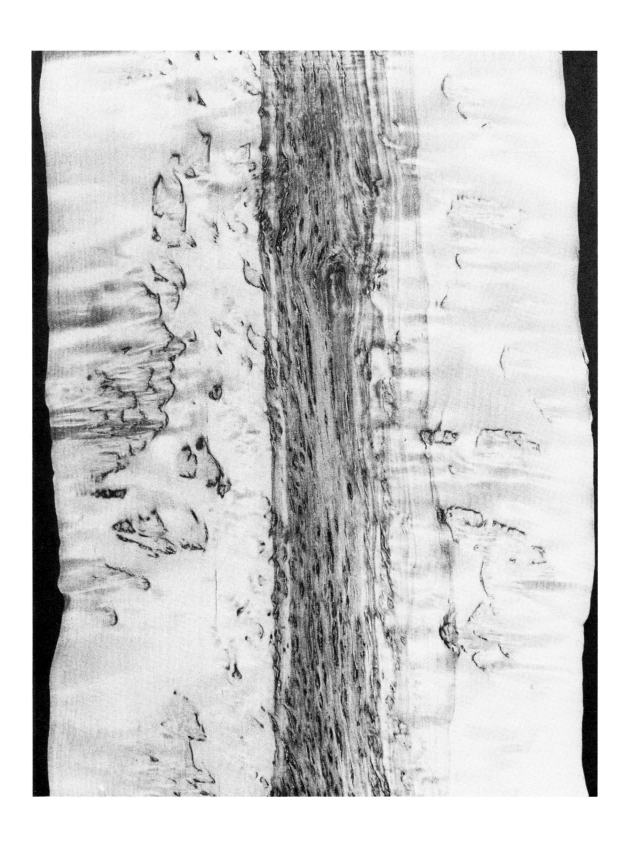

# JAMES KRENOV WORKER IN WOOD

VAN NOSTRAND REINHOLD COMPANY
New York   Cincinnati   Toronto   London   Melbourne

Printed in the United States of America
Photographs by Bengt Carlén
Design by Jean Callan King/Visuality

Published by Van Nostrand Reinhold Company
135 West 50th Street, New York, NY 10020

Van Nostrand Reinhold Limited
1410 Birchmount Road
Scarborough, Ontario M1P 2E7, Canada

Van Nostrand Reinhold Australia Pty. Ltd.
17 Queen Street
Mitcham, Victoria 3132, Australia

Van Nostrand Reinhold Company Limited
Molly Millars Lane
Wokingham, Berkshire, England

16  15  14  13  12  11  10  9  8  7  6  5  4  3  2  1

**Library of Congress Cataloging in Publication Data**
Krenov, James.
   James Krenov, worker in wood.

   Includes index.
   1. Cabinet-work.  2. Krenov, James.  I.  Title.
TT197.K67      684.1′04      80-22185
ISBN 0-442-26336-8

# Acknowledgments

With each book attempted my own efforts become less important, while those of friends assume more just proportions. This time there would have been no book at all were it not for persons who, knowing the complex odds against their being able to see at first hand work such as mine, asked for the next best thing: a closer look at photographs. These had to be painstakingly gathered, and it again became the lot of Bengt Carlén to do the job. As one who has tried and failed, I am aware now of the sheer effort, patience, and skill behind photography such as Carlén's. I trust this appreciation will be shared by others.

Throughout all the later stages of the book, Nancy N. Green and Barbara Kelman-Burgower gave encouragement as well as the benefit of their experience. Jean Callan King did the design—with sensitivity for all concerned.

To Craig McArt and Donald L. McKinley go silent thanks: Their own words will, I hope, be taken as relating to more than any one book or single craftsman.

# Contents

# Foreword

There have been milestones of influence along the way—the Arts and Crafts Movement, the Danish Cabinetmakers Guild—all helping to preserve the revered tradition of individual woodcraft in the age of industrialization. For the modern woodworker, however, no influence has been so profound as the recent acceptance of the craft as a creative art form worthy of critical attention from galleries, museums, and the press.

Once this happened, it subjected woodcraft to the vagaries of the contemporary art market. Pressures from gallery directors and museum curators challenged craftsmen to produce novel pieces that would excite viewers and tickle their fancies. If the works proved to be controversial or even bizarre to the point of offending traditional values, so much the better.

Art critics who found the new developments in woodcraft refreshing praised the innovative efforts of individuals they now most appropriately called artist-craftsmen. They lent encouragement to a movement and expansion in the craft that ultimately penetrated the bounds of sculpture. There, at last, they could assess the work at face value—as form without preoccupation with craftsmanship. Cursory tributes to finish or color could be made without demanding an understanding of the nature of the material or explaining the complexities of the joinery. While elevating the craftsman's work to the status of contemporary art, the critics evaluated it in the idiom of its time.

How did all this affect the craftsmen? They were subjected to extraordinary demands to professionalize their approach. As competition among craftsmen intensified, personal styles were perfected and the best were imitated. Promotion became an essen-

tial ingredient in establishing a reputation, and only a reputation could guarantee any measure of economic success and security. A certain business acumen was required—the ability to rationalize production through planning and systematization, employment of assistants and agents, purchase of machinery and facilities, and so on. Some knowledge of marketing, pricing, and distribution was deemed especially important. These kinds of concerns were reflected in craft school programs, which stressed businesslike professionalism as fundamental to the artist-craftsman's training. The craftsman evolved not only as an artist, a cultivated personality, but also as an entrepreneur capable of managing his own small business.

How this should be taken is a matter of opinion. The fact is that the craft of woodworking has, at least in modest terms, flourished in recent times—an anomaly of sorts in this era of high technology and mass production. The single program established at the School for American Craftsmen in 1945 produced not only artist-craftsmen, but teachers who subsequently introduced recognizable versions of their own training in numerous programs elsewhere. Gallery, museum, and press interest in woodcraft has increased slowly but steadily. One might perceive that, indeed, there exists in the eighties a solid establishment of these modern craftsmen in wood.

Almost neglected in this rush to embrace the productive have been the true "amateurs." These are the many—surprisingly many—woodworkers who choose to pursue their craft primarily for the pleasure and satisfaction they derive from it. They may be unwilling to make compromises to compete in the establishment, or they may simply wish to enjoy an avocation that provides an almost spiritual fulfillment in its pursuit. These craftsmen are likely to view the very opportunities for achieving notoriety in their craft as imposing limitations that would dampen their enthusiasm for their work.

In this context the term *amateur* does not imply any lack of expertise. The amateur woodworkers may work more modestly, but, released from the pressures of maintaining production volume and the like, they are able to uphold values of integrity

and quality that result from time, care, and harmony in the doing. The rewards from this kind of approach are mostly personal: a quiet sense of enjoyment and pride, seldom any notoriety. Because these craftsmen are by choice so inconspicuous, constituting, if you will, a silent majority of woodworkers, they are easily, and sometimes conveniently, overlooked.

With the arrival of James Krenov's *A Cabinetmaker's Notebook* in 1976, followed by *The Fine Art of Cabinetmaking* (1977) and *The Impractical Cabinetmaker* (1979), these individuals found real encouragement from a master craftsman who championed the very same values they held. Not only was there encouragement in Krenov's message, there was advice and, above all, deep understanding of the personal choices they had made. From far and wide came the inquiries: Who is this man? How could they reach him? They were anxious to communicate, to let him know that they had been touched by his sincerity or had been inspired by his example. And they turned up in increasing numbers to hear him lecture and to participate in workshops. For as much as he is a master craftsman, he is a master teacher, able to coax forth the best in each student.

Krenov's message is a simple one and a poetic one. It starts with respect for the wood. He dwells on the mystery of this living material,

the different species from far corners of the world, and the decisions that will determine its final form —decisions in which the wood itself should have a determining voice. And there is respect also for the tools, whether they be planes and knives that one fashions for himself or light machinery that is tuned to dependable cooperation. Whatever the tool, it must extend the user's control and never control the user. For in the work, the doing, there must be harmony. This is the crux of the message, and without it the result will suffer. It places prime importance on an intuitive feel for what is right, and it stresses attitudes of curiosity and virtues of integrity. Above all, it makes a promise: that the pleasure is in the doing. It follows, therefore, that tangible evidence of that pleasure will be in the piece thus made.

Krenov has lived with his family in Sweden and worked alone in a small shop in his home. He studied cabinetmaking in Stockholm when he traveled there from the United States and stayed on after the war. The traditional training he received has perhaps influenced his work more than he will admit. Not that his work is traditional, but the discipline and thoroughness are a part of him and are consequently ingrained in his approach. His love for the wood and his attitude toward work may well have developed through childhood experiences growing up among people who used skilled hands—in a remote Alaskan village and, later, on Puget Sound, where he helped build and repair wooden boats.

Although the Swedish social system has been favorable to artists and craftsmen, one finds parochial attitudes about woodworking and an isolation from the mainstream of this craft that are frustrating and difficult to overcome. Typically, cabinetmakers in Scandinavia work in production shops crafting furniture according to drawings created by designers. The level of craftsmanship may be high, but there is little demand for creativity or individual expression. Krenov has been very much alone in Sweden as a cabinetmaker who regards the conception and the realization of a piece as a single, personal effort.

During the seventies, his teaching and lecturing in North America and Europe brought him into contact with a much wider and more appreciative public. His books on cabinetmaking have found an enthusiastic readership around the world.

This book is about Krenov's work. Our appreciation of his work is enriched by a comprehension of how each piece came to be: the intent, the inspiration, the risks that were taken, and the discoveries that were made along the way. There are subtleties in Krenov's work that want understanding and offer a reward for those who look closely and *feel*. Krenov's form language is modest and refined. He regards himself as a cabinetmaker, a

traditional term. His work, in fact, consists almost exclusively of cabinets, cases, and tables. Now, in his sixties, he is perhaps at the prime of his capabilities, experienced and confident in his approach, still physically able to manage the rigors of handling heavy planks of wood, and in firm control of the sensitivity that matches the will of his mind with the skill of his hands. The level of quality he attains through uncompromising control of all aspects of his work is, in itself, uncommon. But, transcending the craftsmanship, one senses the spirit and soul of an extraordinary man.

Craig McArt
ROCHESTER INSTITUTE OF TECHNOLOGY
ROCHESTER, NEW YORK

JAMES KRENOV WORKER IN WOOD

# The Size of Objects

I have been reminded that photographs can mislead one as to the sizes of the objects themselves, especially when there is nothing to compare them with. Most of the work I do is fairly small. This is partly because wood to me is precious, and very often I have planks with parts that contain something that interests me and may lead to a certain piece being made. Also, my shop is small, with rather unprofessional equipment; it is difficult for me to join and surface wide stock. And finally, by my nature I have a tendency toward detailed work. There is a dimension beyond which I feel I will accomplish less rather than more.

The largest object in this book, the no-glass showcase cabinet done in lemon wood and doussie, is barely six feet tall. The curved-front cherry wood cabinet is just over five and one-half feet high and less than two and one-half feet wide. None of the other objects is what one might call heavy or imposing. The cabinet of padouk with the odd panels in the doors is only three feet wide and four and one-half feet high. The others, mostly wall cabinets, are what I suppose one could call hold-in-the-hand objects. They are easy to carry and to mount in place. They are not heavy, and I hope they have a light look. I imagine them as being something one would like to hold (or discover with one's hands).

Lately I have had the urge to work very minutely, to decrease the scale of my work even further. I do not know whether this is because my supply of precious wood is dwindling and I am not replenishing it since I am no longer young, or that I simply am physically less able to handle the large planks I have had and cherished for so many years.

# Cabinet of

# Andaman Padouk

About eight or nine years ago I had a memorable experience. I was invited by one of my wood suppliers to come down to the mill in southern Sweden and be present when they opened—that is to say, made the first cut in—a log of Andaman padouk. It was an old part of the mill, and they had an ancient, horizontal band saw to which the log came creaking on a wooden cradle. The whole atmosphere was of another time. The saw blade hissed, and from this dirty gray log came a spray of rich orange sawdust. Then the dogs bit the upper half of the log, lifted it free—and there were marvelous, glowing colors, rippling orange and crimson. Not only did it affect me, a sentimental fellow about wood, but even the old-timers who were present during the sawing smiled a little.

I had them cut a few flitches for me, and, since it is unfair to take only the best part of the log and leave the outer cuts to the mill, I agreed to take

some of these too, fairly narrow planks with part of the sapwood and the first of the reddish color, which in this case was much lighter than the rich red farther inside the log. For quite a few years I had these planks of Andaman padouk with two definite colors, mostly dark red and a few orange.

In 1978 and 1979, I was in what one might call a curves period, making cabinets with convex and concave surfaces, some showcases but mostly pieces with solid wood doors. Suddenly I wanted to make a curved front cabinet, concave, fairly large, out of this padouk. The first thought of the panels in the doors being the same curve as the door frames themselves was not enough to excite me; I groped further. Then it occurred to me: panels having a greater curve than the framed parts of the doors themselves! With this thought came the almost obvious idea that the panels should be made out of the lighter padouk, the rest of

the cabinet of the darker. Now the dark part of the log farther inside was definitely rowed wood, almost impossible to plane. I had to rough plane the contours of the sides, for example, and then work them with cabinet scrapers and finally sand and polish them. But the wood just under the sapwood at the outside of the log had the grain on the flat; the rowed fibers were not obvious, nor were they a hindrance to planing. I was able to plane the final curved surfaces of these panels both inside and out. The cabinet came about in a somewhat backward manner as far as method is concerned. I had a rough idea of the size, I knew the body should be fairly high up off the floor, but as yet I did not know more. My attention was fixed on the doors; I was convinced that the cabinet would succeed or fail depending on how good the doors were with their panels. So I worked on these. One might say I built the rest of the cabinet around the doors.

There is not much to reflect on in the way of technical difficulties. This is not a complicated piece, but I think if one is to do such work and enjoy it, there has to be a sense of sequence; one has to find a flow, follow one's feelings, the images that come and go. And rely on logic from step to step. I talk very often about this, and sometimes with young people I may spend three or four weeks, at the end of which the only thing we have accomplished is the state of being more relaxed about ourselves and our work. We are not as intimidated as we were before about certain technical ABCs and all kinds of laborsaving methods and a sort of rigidness that is not easy for different kinds of people to adapt themselves to.

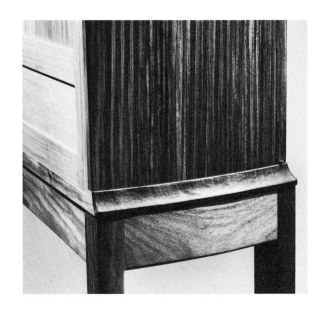

One thing led to another as the cabinet grew. The lengthwise piece down near the floor, the curve joining the two side stretchers between the legs, was not pleasant at first, cut as it was equally thick and to a shape representing the front curve of the cabinet. The back of the cabinet, however, was straight. . . . There was a contradiction that led me to reshape the piece by means of a gradual bevel that left its upper edge thinner at the middle and lessened the sense of curve along the back. This was pleasant and obviously made sense. Though, honestly, the obvious did not emerge until after I had done something that did not feel right.

*The piece is oil treated outside, except for door panels, which are waxed to accentuate the color difference. The door handles are of cocobolo. Inside, the cabinet is polished—a very thin coating of shellac and alcohol applied at least four times. The drawer fronts are of steamed pear wood, the rest of the drawers are of fragrant Lebanon cedar.*

*Total height, approximately 160cm; width at back, 92cm; at front, 83cm. Completed in 1979.*

The piece needs to be viewed "on the move"; no photograph can give the actual sense of how the shapes and shadings and details change as one walks past the cabinet or views it from various angles—especially under different conditions of lighting. Andaman padouk, the only true padouk, is marvelous in the way it reacts immediately to the slightest change of light, whether daylight or artificial. It is a very, very living wood, even without having exciting patterns. There is a depth and a glow to it, refractions that respond beautifully to light and to shapes that are not rigid. One should remember: Some woods do have this quality of being enriched by certain shapes and certain lighting. The wood itself is not an unchanging pattern or color, but it lives with light. Part of the enjoyment of things made of such wood is exactly this richness. So what we see here is not so much to the credit of this cabinetmaker as it is of someone infinitely more important.

# Wall Cabinet
# of English Brown Oak

To me, English brown oak is not at its best in flat surfaces or even in large, unbroken areas. But it is fine wood. Besides, it responds so well to my planes. This concave door has an asymmetrical curve, which in a sense wanted to bend out away from the wall on what turned out to be its left. Since a handle would, I felt, be disturbing, the door has a lip along its right edge. Consequently, opening the door from right to left feels more comfortable than if it were otherwise.

The drawers are simply for fun (or to break the possible monotony of dark wood inside the cabinet). They are from the very last bits of some Swedish chestnut that I had kept for nearly twenty years.

*Height, 76cm; width at back, approximately 35cm; at front, 31cm (the left side of the cabinet being set at an angle). Waxed outside, inside has been left untreated. 1977.*

# Box for Berndt Fridberg's Ceramic Pieces

We have in Sweden a much revered ceramist called Berndt Fridberg. He is a modest, down-to-earth person with large hands, and yet the best of his work are tiny stoneware pieces with exquisite glazings and shapes. Fridberg is an elderly man now, and he has been making these pieces for years, so there are many collectors of Fridberg stoneware. One collector was the late King Gustav of Sweden. For the king's seventieth birthday, Berndt Fridberg and the ceramics manufacturer where he has his studio decided to present His Majesty with a box for his collection of stoneware miniatures. I was asked to make the box. The only directive given me was a layout of how His Majesty wanted to arrange the various pieces in the box; in other words, the size and position of the miniatures themselves.

The box is of Swedish maple, very simple. And I recall, though this was some years ago, the thrill of being asked to do such a piece. I remember also the feeling of harmony with which I worked, because this is the kind of detailed work I at times enjoy so much: every choice of wood has its meaning and the way the smallest edge is rounded or a shape is done will be important to someone. I knew His Majesty had a very keen eye not only for the details of Fridberg's stoneware, but also for pottery of the Sung dynasty. He would certainly scrutinize this box. Rather than making me afraid and worried, this added to the simple enjoyment of working.

One does have certain ambitions and the need for appreciation. Is this mere ego, self-assertion—and is it wrong? Is appreciation—secretly now—also recognition? Fairly late in this life I ask myself the question. I have been thumbing through *The Unknown Craftsman,* by Sōetsu Yanagi. The potters of Sung were, I feel, neither recognizable nor totally anonymous. They did emerge in their work. I would like to believe that their being was part of their creating, even if there was no con-scious awareness of this. They sim-ply lived and labored.

However much I wish it, I cannot achieve such obviousness. Only at my work (when it is going as it should) am I serene. Then I am *a* craftsman—no more, no less. While the work envelops me with its ageless truth, this is enough. The work done, another reality imposes itself and I must meet it. At such a time it is good not to feel alone. Watching young people find reas-surance in discovering new sides of their craft and of themselves has helped me realize this. They have gathered, shared generously, and learned much. Feeling they are neither alone nor misled, these craftsmen will find it natural to be concerned first with making some-thing that is their best—and only then facing the problems of how to sell it. Unknown they may be, but they do have friends. They will get help; their work, too, will find friends. In this respect at least, we are improving on the past.

I did not see the box for about fifteen years, until it appeared at the National Museum in Stockholm, in an exhibition of Fridberg's work. The maple has aged very well, and the box has been used with care; it has been appreciated. I feel this — and a satisfaction in the fact that the stoneware pieces, these lovely things Fridberg has done, are in a sense a part of the box. Everything together is a whole, putting my work in a proper relationship to that of other people and other experiences. It makes me less apt to regard my part — that is to say the piece, whether it is a cabinet or a box like this — as the ultimate goal.

*The size of the box may be deceptive since the stoneware miniatures vary from 3.5cm to 10cm in height. The box is about 45cm long, 31cm wide, and 10cm high. It is finished with oil outside, polish inside, 1964 or 1965.*

# Cabinet of
# Spalted Maple

I suppose most of us who work with a particular material have at one time or another done variations on a certain theme. Such is the case with this cabinet, of which I had previously made three. Of these, I liked each one in its own way and yet, at the end of having made them, something of a question mark was left in my mind. One day, while going through a stack of wood, I got the urge to do one more of these cabinets, which someone originally called ballet dancer.

I had done one in English brown oak and two in pear wood, and by now I had a strong feeling that this particular piece would be at its best when it is rather ethereal, soft in its visual appeal. Among the planks I considered were some spalted maple. I opened up several parts of a large plank and discovered treasures. At one point, where I cut what I thought could be a pair of doors, the pattern was in itself very beautiful, but somehow *too* obvious. And in the spalted pattern was a sloping curve; in other words, whichever way I turned the two parts of the door, there was a disturbing taper. More sawing until I found a very calm, grayish, lightly spalted maple piece, thick enough for doors. Also wood for the sides. All fairly calm but not dull.

*The entire body is maple, to the outside of which a very thin coat of polish has been applied, followed by "Renaissance" wax. The inside is polished. Drawer fronts are of Indian laurel; the rest of the drawers are Lebanon cedar. The door handles are secupira, as is the stand, which has been left untreated.*

*Total height, about 147cm; width at back, 43cm; at front, approximately 36cm. Winter of 1979.*

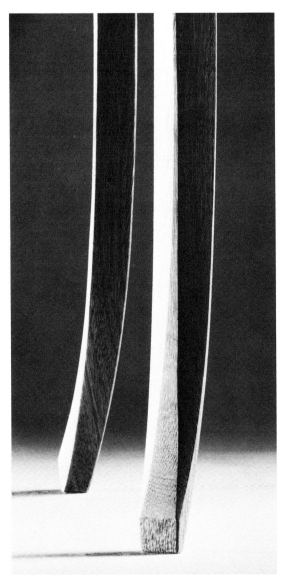

I had, as I got the urge to make this cabinet, an idea that the legs now would be different, more "dancy" than the previous ones. Those had a curve at the base, the lower end being the thickest part of each leg, the back pair of which stood almost at right angles to the cabinet sides. Now, however, I would make legs whose ends tapered toward the floor; in other words, this cabinet would really be on its toes.

What wood for the stand? Simply oak—too light. Brown oak—no. Walnut—liable to have too much pattern of its own. Secupira now—this thick plank, yes! Both the case and the stand would have a soft, misty texture. I am sure my feeling of texture in these woods was very important and had a strong effect upon every aspect of the result.

In doing the previous pieces I had learned something about both cabinet and stand. The cabinet case *by itself* should not take up all one's attention in the way of proportions. It should not be beautifully proportioned because it is not the entire piece. Only when the stand is made does the final balance emerge. A good proportion for the same cabinet if it is made as a wall-hung piece is not ideal here. I had to allow for the stand and deliberately, almost grudgingly, make the cabinet itself a

little bit shorter than I might want to. So, having put together the carcase with the doors roughly formed, I worked on the stand.

Shaping parts of this was a matter of patience, because secupira is a rock-hard South American wood, rowed and very difficult to work with hand tools. What I did was come as close as I could in my imagination to the shape and size of the legs. Then I made a small template of the main curve—that is to say, the leg as seen from the side—after which I drew, freehand, using my thumb as a guide, the various bevels, slightly twisted, that finally give the leg its shape. I band-sawed all four legs almost to their final dimensions, getting a good deal of satisfaction out of this. It appealed to my vanity somehow, being able to saw by eye and feel, following a rough line while cutting even closer to my *intention,* knowing that I was achieving a shape only with the saw. There would be as little as possible of unnecessary handwork afterwards. Yes, I needed to plane a bit, and file and scrape and finally polish the legs. But I kept from being so far off in my initial shapes that there would be an un-necessary amount of hard labor. Because then, tiring oneself out and getting a bit irritated, one is apt to

lose clarity of vision and steadiness of hand—and perhaps even the sense of the shape that is wanted.

The legs are set at angles different from those I chose earlier; the "hind" ones are angled back a bit, which means I really did not think it necessary for the cabinet to stand against a wall. Why should it? It is a very free piece with a will of its own, and it should have the space and the chance to dance.

The stand done, I finished the case

with its curves. The maple is rather soft, very silky, wonderful to plane. It calls for *visual softness,* which accounts for the shape of the top piece and perhaps some of the details of the corners and edges.

Inside, the way the pattern of the maple relates to the right-hand drawer is pure coincidence; but afterwards, when one looks at it, this adds to the enjoyment. As do the odd reddish splashes at the upper part of the back panel.

There are two other details worth noticing. I wanted the stretchers between the legs to appear fairly thin as seen from above; the stand should feel light. At the same time, I needed the structural strength of still another thickness. So I beveled the upper inside edge of each stretcher. Result: The part you see is a bit thinner than the total thickness.

Finally, there is the back piece of the stand, with its lower edge curved slightly upwards. As one looks at the cabinet from the front, or nearly front, that back piece is partly visible. If it were a straight line, it would conflict with the front curves of both cabinet and stand. I have shaped the underside of the back piece so that just as it appears between the two front stretchers it has a curve coinciding with these.

Then, as you raise your point of view and the back stretcher is about to disappear below the bottom front edge of the cabinet, the two curves join. Most people would not even notice this. They would take it for granted, which is as it should be. There is, of course, the built-in risk that if the back piece were left straight and stiff someone might take *that* for granted, too. . . .

# Details

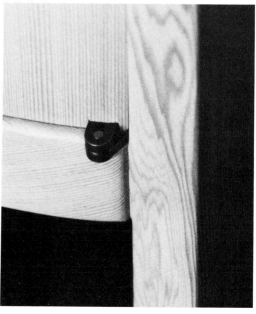

# No-Glass Showcase
# of Lemon Wood

This goes back about fifteen years, to a time when I found some lemon wood exceptional in its beauty and clarity, and also the first doussie wood I was able to get here in Sweden.

All the main surfaces of the cabinet, the top, bottom, and "platform," are veneered. This veneer I cut on my band saw to a thickness of slightly over one-sixteenth of an inch, the same veneer on both sides of each surface. The cabinet being fairly large by my standards, there was a great deal of dust and noise and simply hard labor in this process. Also, I had very limited facilities for gluing such surfaces. But I was younger then, optimistic, and with a surplus of energy, and I do not remember this cabinet as being painful in the sense of hard work. It was something entirely new for me. I made it in one sweep. And although many years later I did another cabinet based on the same idea, which may or may not be better, I still look back upon this one and the experience that went with it, not only without regrets, but with a certain nostalgia, the sense that perhaps today I could not manage such a complex and time-consuming piece.

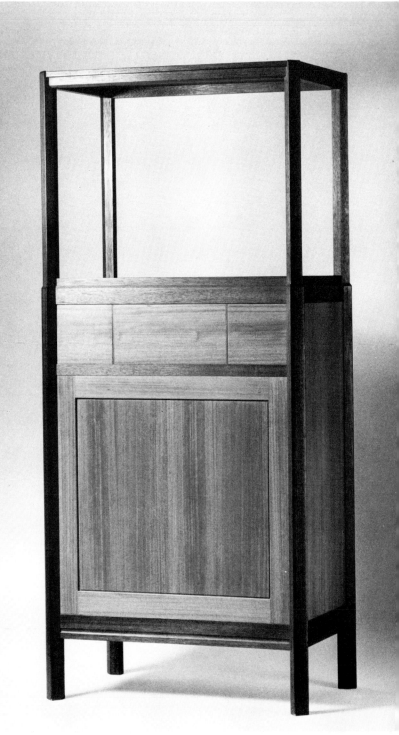

48

Two "secret" compartments are made accessible by removing a drawer on the corresponding side, lifting a catch, and then pivoting open the back "door." All this was not a part of planning the cabinet, but came about simply because I did not think its front would be pleasing with three drawers, side by side. Nor did I want the drawers wider than they are. The result: a space on either side and the feeling that someone might ask what it is for.

Perhaps, too, I was a bit influenced by what sometimes happened in the more elaborate apprentice pieces made at cabinetmakers' schools in the (good?) old days. All sorts of ingenious ways were found to in-clude *somewhere* a hidden compart-ment. False back pieces or extra drawer bottoms would reveal their contents—from a will to currency to mere dust—years later, if ever. . . .

*Height, 157cm; width, 62cm; depth, approximately 33cm. Polished inside and outside (very thin coat applied five or six times). 1962.*

# Writing Table
# of Italian Walnut

Some ideas simply impose themselves; there is no originality or design involved. Which is a relief to craftsmen like me. When I write, I twist to the left—a straight-edged table is not ideal. On the assumption that someone else might have the same problem, I wanted to make a table such as this. It took the wood to get me started: A plank of wonderful Italian walnut had the curve and the taper that said, "Here it is!"

This is a once-only piece, at least in walnut, since I am not very fond of American walnut and the finest European variety is almost extinct. Besides, European or American (whatever its nationality) walnut with this particular pattern and delicate color does not simply grow on trees.

Length at back, 98cm; curved front edge,
78cm; left-side end, 72cm wide; right-side
end, 48.5cm wide; total height, 75cm. Wax
finish. 1977.

# Cabinet of
# Old Swedish Elm

The flared sides are about one and
three-quarter inches thick at the base
and nearly as thick along the top,
carved edge. The doors are shaped to
compound curves, coopered and
hand-planed so each door edge meets
a side of the cabinet.

*Height, 135cm; width at base, 53cm; at top,
52cm; maximum depth, approximately
23.5 cm. Waxed outside. 1977–1978.*

# Bits of Maple
# Wall Cabinet

There seem to be two rather definite views regarding this object. People either like it or do not take to it at all. When one of the elderly and much-respected critics here in Stockholm came into our room and saw it, she simply sniffed: "Krenov should not make things like that!" And yet there have been others who have said, "Well, is it the only such you have made?" Some have wanted either to have me make something similar for them or to purchase this particular one. But I have kept it, probably because I have never been quite sure whether it was a success or a failure—or something in between. Here it is, for whatever it's worth. I can well imagine someone else taking up this simple idea, doing something quite different and much more interesting.

All the wood in the cabinet is maple. Some of it Swedish, some from America, some from the heartwood; parts are in the early stages of spalting or being affected by other changes. I merely wanted to do such a piece, without any deep philosophical contemplation as to how the door should be given "meaning." I rather enjoyed sawing and carving the little blocks and then putting them together with wooden pegs. I also had fun painting it inside—first several coats of titanium white, then one thin layer of green oil paint, which I mixed myself.

*Height, approximately 82cm; width, 21cm; depth, 13cm. Oil finish outside except for small pieces in door, which are left untreated. 1962.*

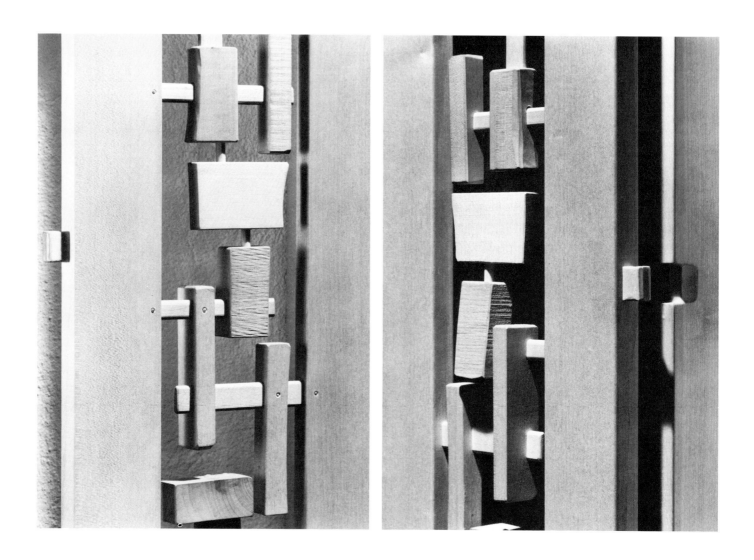

*Detail of door from the inside shows wooden pegs holding the various shaped pieces in place.*

# Details

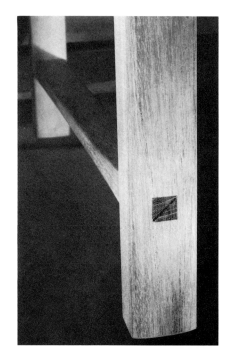

# Wall Cabinet of Maple

This cabinet is of spalted maple that some of my young friends sent me from America. The wood is sound, there is no rot, though there is a good deal of the spalted effect from moisture and fungus. The rough-cut plank as it was chain-sawed showed only small wormholes. Then, when I got into it, I discovered in working the surfaces that with each of these little wormholes was a reddish-brown streak. Quite fascinating, it added to the appeal of the wood, which, besides the soft color, wormholes, and traces of fungus, had a luster when it was planed or cut with sharp tools of any kind.

I had sawn the main stock for the cabinet, pieces for the doors, top, bottom, and sides, and had these propped against a wall of my shop when, one day, I heard the sound of heavy boots on the stairs outside, followed by a banging on the door. In walked a rather young man with an outdoor look about him. "I am

with the forest service and I have just done a thesis on badgers," he said to me. "I thought I'd drop in." Then he saw these pieces of maple, walked up to them, and scrutinized each.

"Hey, you know what these little holes are?"

"Yes," I said. "Someone has been living there, obviously."

"That's right," he nodded. "But I'll tell you: These little creatures who lived here," he pointed to one of the wormholes, "go out and gather the mold culture as food for their offspring, and later this contributes to the fungus spreading through the wood."

He was a nice chap, and he gave me a fine description of badgers from the time they are very small until they grow up, together with a beautiful photograph of one of his badger friends. Now each time I look at this little cabinet I think not only of him, but of wood one could describe as ecological.

*Height, 73cm; width, 24cm; depth, about
13cm. The drawer is rosewood, the door
handle of Macassar ebony. The piece is
waxed outside, with the inside lightly
polished. 1977.*

# Music Stand

This is the first of four I have made and the only one with the slats placed vertically. (Notice they become narrower toward the outsides of the frames.)

*The dimensions of the folding stand itself are partiture (score) size, about 68cm by 41cm. Total height with stand raised is 105cm. The lemon wood is oil finished. 1963.*

# Only in Ash?

This piece disproves something I stated in my earliest book. I have done this type of cabinet about four times during the ten years or so since I made the first one. Always in ash. The reason, I think, was that not only did the delicacy of ash seem to be a part of the mood in which I conceived the piece, but also that I had a particularly fine pattern in the back panel of the first cabinet (and the succeeding ones). I firmly believed that the cabinet should always be of ash and that it always should contain such a pattern in order to give it the rhythm I thought was its main asset. The years went by and, until rather recently, I did not make the cabinet at all because I did not have any ash with *the* suitable pattern for the back panels. After I made the large cabinet of Andaman padouk with its peculiar curves, I had some pieces of padouk left. Among these were thin cuts that revealed interesting knots and whorls in the wood. For some reason it occurred to me to give the showcase a try. I had never seen it in dark wood,

and there was something special about these pieces for the back panels, so why not try? I did the cabinet, and here it is. I believe that in a way—if one does not compare too closely or if one has not lived with one of the cabinets in ash—this cabinet by itself is not inferior to any of them. In fact, I think it has a flavor of its own. I can imagine that in a particular environment it may be even more stimulating or exciting than a cabinet in ash.

So the meaning, or sense moral, is simply that not only am I unsure as a craftsman but, like most of us, I have tendencies and concepts about things I imagine to be certainties that, in fact, change through the years. I should be grateful for this kind of stimulus based on questioning and little discoveries usually made through the wood itself. In other words, having a particular piece of a new kind of wood and associating it with a cabinet or other item one has done suddenly poses questions. And one does want to know at least some of the answers.

*The cabinet in ash.*

*Height, 69cm; width, 44.5cm; maximum depth, 17cm. Wax finish outside, polish inside. 1979.*

# Pipe Cabinet

I used to smoke a pipe. Mostly I did this while out walking. No doubt because long ago, as a boy in Alaska, I often went hunting with my father, whose Indian-like walk and silent awareness when in the woods left a deep impression on me. I guess his pipe somehow belonged to the image, which was an outdoor one.

Years later, in Sweden, when getting ready for a stroll, I would light my one pipe, a battered meerschaum. "Here you are, going out for some fresh air—and you're going to smoke all the way," my wife would chide. Finally that started to make sense. After a while, I stopped smoking. The pipe is still around, though—as a mellow remembrance.

Well, when I needed to make a pipe cabinet for a certain person, I had help from an old, bad habit. The construction of the door emerged from the need for constant ventilation. I knew how a pipe or pipes smell if kept in a closed place. Also, I was aware of how much one putters with a pipe besides smoking it. Hence the removable racks.

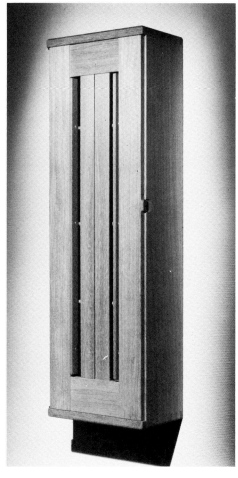

*Height, 86cm; width, 26cm; depth, approximately 14cm. The case is of English brown oak, the drawer and removable pipe racks are of rosewood. Both woods are untreated. 1968.*

# Table for
# a Chinese Horse

A Swedish gentleman was invited to China on a cultural visit. He found a reproduction porcelain horse, good—though the original would have been priceless—and he managed to keep it intact during various hectic legs of his travels.

At home, it stood uncertainly on a sideboard. When he suggested we provide a better place for it, I responded—partly to him, a bit to the horse, and certainly because I had just the wood that would please them both: East Indian rosewood and Indian laurel. The laurel panel is set low in the rosewood frame so the horse, though it can pivot a bit, cannot slide off.

*A cross-piece is fitted to support the panel. This is merely a precaution, since the panel is a safe three-eighths of an inch thick.*

# Game Box

A friend in a Swedish city north of where I live sent me a letter tucked inside a smallish package. He has a sense of humor, and the letter began with, "This has got to be one of the strangest requests you have ever received." It was. Arne enjoys playing an ancient game called Vira, which is why the package contained a deck of cards, a small starter's pistol plus blank cartridges, a scorecard, and something resembling a teacher's bell such as has been long out of use.

"I'd like you to make a box for all this," Arne wrote. "Something easy to carry. . . . I get together with a few cronies about once a month, and we play Vira. You never heard of it? Well, that's part of the laugh—neither have a lot of other people. It's an almost forgotten game."

The resulting box is of perobinha wood (from South America); the panel in the sliding lid is spalted boxwood, probably from Asia via London and left over from a clock I made six or seven years ago. The four lower corners are related in a way similar to those of my chessboard (pages 96 and 97): The two side pieces of the box have been raised a trifle, the end pieces cut in a slight upward bow on the underside, allowing the box to rest steadily.

Neither of these woods would be at its best oiled, so I treated the outside of the box with wax, leaving the inside natural.

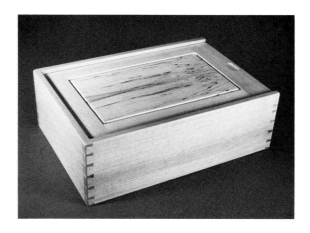 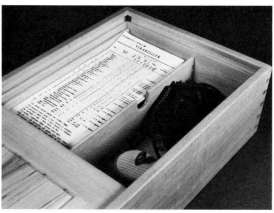

*Length, about 30cm; width, 22cm; height, 11cm. 1979.*

# Details

# Kitchen Cabinet

This was for a friend. He headed a team building supertankers and does silversmithing as a hobby. Through the years he acquired several of my pieces. When he asked me to do this one, we were both relaxed—it was a fun thing. He told me what he'd have in it and the rest was up to me. The wood is wirola (as the old man at the yard where I found it years ago called it). It took a fine oil finish.

When I visit my friend Einar, we dine at the kitchen table. The cabinet is on the wall behind where he usually chooses to sit. Sometimes, between sips of wine, he turns around, then looks at me, smiles— and winks.

*Total width, approximately 80cm; height, 57cm; depth, 15cm. 1976.*

# Violin Cabinet

This was done for a musician in the Stockholm Philharmonic Orchestra. She came to me with a Guarneri violin and the simple statement that it was *not* a showpiece; she used it almost daily and wanted it easy to reach, together with the bow and resin, in a fitting cabinet. What cabinet could ever do justice to that Guarneri! Of course I did not succeed, except in the sense that the result pleases Mrs. Gilblad, who is a fine musician and loves her instrument.

*Height, 55cm; width, 88cm; depth, 23cm. The case is of Oregon pine, the horizontal door panels of larch wood, the handles of pear wood, and the sliding trays of beechwood. Oil finish on the outside, the inside left natural. 1969.*

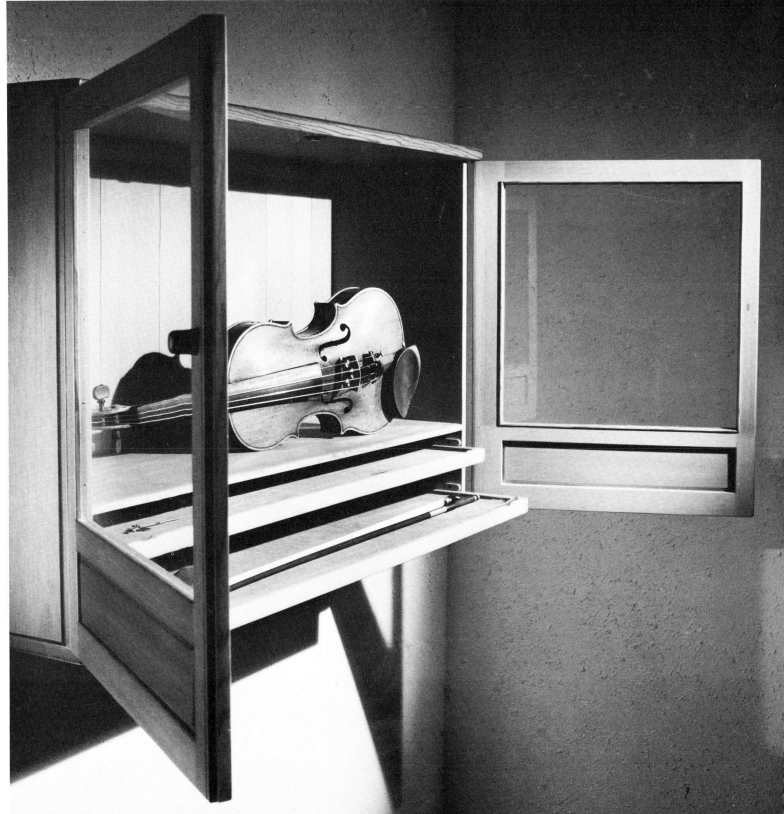

# Showcase of Ash

It is sometimes difficult to find a balance between wood and glass in a piece like this one. I had help from the mild, straight-grained ash. But what brought things together was the spalted maple. These panel pieces, unlike other, grayish maple I had, went very well with the ash. Getting them out of the small, badly checked planks (I had to go through two), I thought of my young friend Olof, now living in the woods of New England, and how much energy there is in such friendships — it was not easy for him to send this wood to me!

*Height, approximately 76cm; width, 43cm; depth, 12 or 13cm. The cabinet is wax finished, since ash does not like a wet-looking finish (such as oil gives). Besides, the maple panels would have been too much darkened by even the mildest oil. The handles are of olive wood. 1978.*

# Chessboard

I made this board after having completed one or two chess tables. The playing surface, entirely of solid wood squares, is doweled together and quite stable in all seasons. It has a space of nearly one-eighth of an inch between the squares. This gives a sense of lightness, a kind of airiness. Also, one can give the squares a hard or soft feeling depending on how the edges and corners are rounded. This work is done separately with each square before the playing surface is glued together.

Notice that on the underside at each corner the two parts of the frame are not flush as they meet. One part has been planed down about one-sixteenth of an inch. This was done after the dovetails were made and dry-fitted. In one direction, where the frame member is thicker, I planed a very slight upward arc by holding the plane horizontally and then angling it a bit as I cut. The plane made its own natural curve. This helps the frame to rest firmly on its four corners.

I do not remember a special sat-

isfaction or a sense of inventiveness after having arrived at this solution. I am very much aware of how we craftsmen are being bombarded by the need for being inventive. Some of us shy away from that part of our craft; forcing details is a strain

on us. But I think details with a purpose—made when one is relaxed, following one's logic, putting oneself into the position of the person who will use the object one is making, and just letting things come—are rewarding in a quiet way.

*Outside dimensions about 48 by 48cm. The doussie frame is 4.5cm high. The playing surface of Rio rosewood and natural pear wood is waxed, the frame oil finished. 1974.*

# Details

# Candlestick

I am not a woodcarver, but some twenty-five years ago, at a cabinet-makers' school, I did not realize this. Carving was done there, and, late evenings on my own time, I made this candlestick of very hard cherry wood. When the old professor saw it, he did not grace it with a comment. Nonetheless, during the next term I was asked to do a two-door cabinet of his design, the panels of which were carved with a garland of flowers in low relief.

*Height, 28cm; maximum diameter, 6cm.*
*The cherry wood is left unfinished. 1956.*

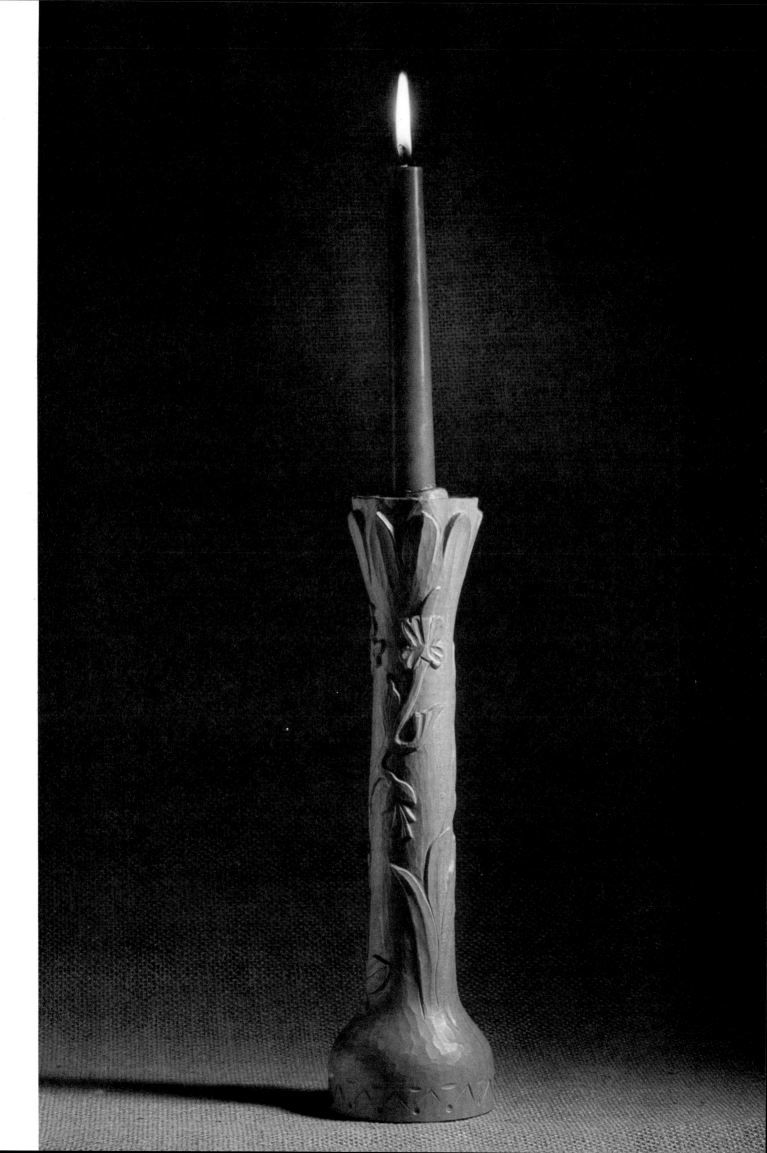

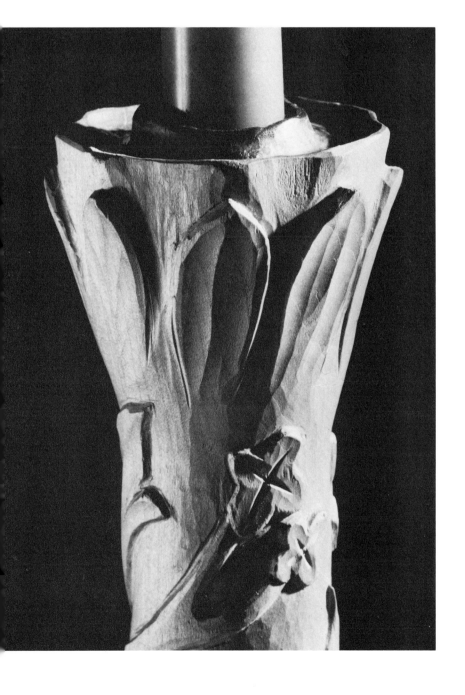

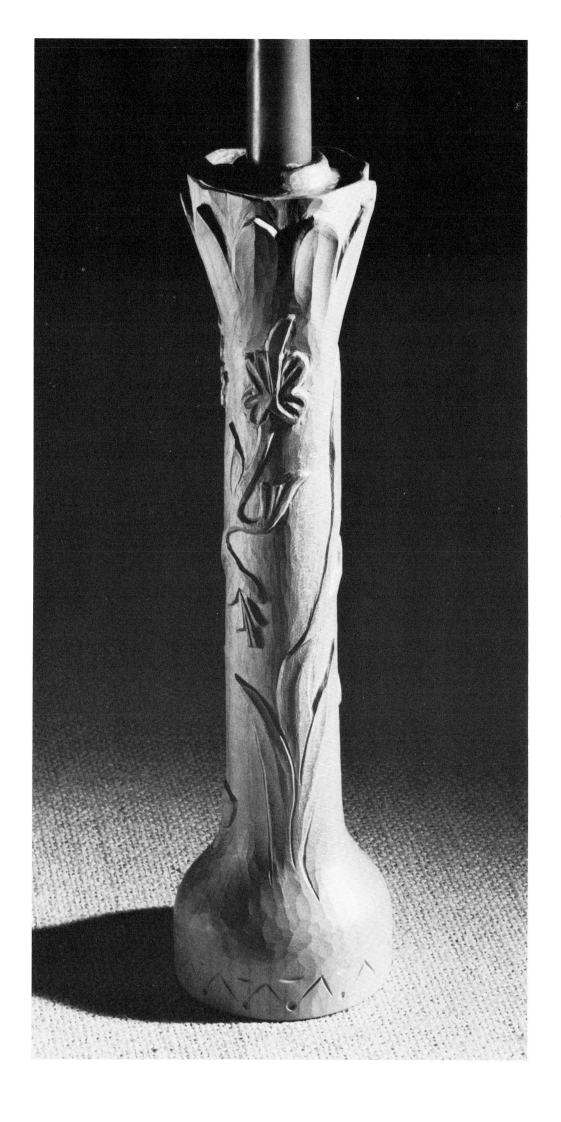

# Showcase of Doussie

This is a predecessor of the more
elaborate showcases with which
I eventually became entangled.
The idea here was simply to try
something with glass in a door that
was not just one unbroken surface. I
wanted to do so especially since real
"live" blown glass is impossible to
find these days. The glass available
now is either a poor imitation of the
old or simply a spotless surface,
whether it reflects a glare or not.

I wanted as much as possible of the
cabinet's inside to be visible, yet the
door, with its joints and the rabbet
for the glass, had to be strong.
Therefore, each of the four corners
has a double slot and tenon; in other
words, the frame members are almost square—"on the flat," really
—instead of the usual wider-than-
thick construction with a single slot
joint at each corner.

The grid is half-lapped, the glass
one piece. Behind each horizontal
wood strip is a glass shelf.

*Height, 86cm; width, 22cm; depth, about
14cm. Oiled outside, untreated inside. About
1970.*

# Showcase Cabinet
# of Cherry Wood

I have chosen this as a working illustration, an example of the way most of the pieces I make come about. This particular one represents not so much technical difficulties or particular details of construction as it does a very basic problem, namely, that however some of us may be able to sketch or imagine things in our mind, there are surprises, and problems, when it comes to the work itself. We may have a fair idea of how we think a piece will look and may even make drawings, yet there are certain aspects in the nature of various forms and proportions—and especially in the material we work with, wood with its own graphic messages—that turn the whole process of working from a matter of certainty, or even rather definite suppositions, to a series of adventures that takes us from one uncertainty to another, with hopes of reaching a turning point. That is exactly what happened during the

making of this particular cabinet. I went through a series of adventures; more by luck than by anything else, I passed a critical point. From then on I made the piece, which, even if I do not regard it as a favorite, is still one I like. There is no need to regret the fact that it is the way it turned out to be—almost despite me.

For a long time I had had an idea for a two-piece, concave-front cabinet, showcase above and paneled doors below, all with soft curves. Only that; I do not think I had a clear notion of anything but the feel of those shapes, in a piece not too big. Light or dark, I was not sure. . . .

*Total height, 170 cm; lower half, with its oak base, is 98 cm high; maximum width at back, 74 cm; at front, approximately 66 cm. Oil finish on entire outside and drawer fronts, interior is polished. Beginning of 1980.*

*A shelf behind and just below the level of the door frame brings objects into full view. In glass, the shelf gives a "floating" effect to whatever rests on it, with the wood of the cabinet bottom still a presence. With a wooden shelf, the feeling is different: the base of the showcase part becomes more solid since one is unaware of the space under the shelf. Note that the figurine shown in the picture is not a Meissen piece, but a Rumanian "stand-in."*

I was working on something else when one day a couple came to see me. They brought some small porcelain figurines. I think really they intended—with the help of these figurines—to somehow convince me that I should do a cabinet for them. And they succeeded. Because these were lovely eighteenth-century Meissen porcelain figures from Dresden, quite enticing.

We talked about the general way in which this cabinet might be used, where it was to be placed. It and the things in it would be viewed from standing-height rather than sitting. Sometimes, of course, from farther on in the room one might look from a sitting position, but not often. The main idea was that the figurines and the cabinet should be pleasant when one stood or moved fairly close to them.

Well, the idea of the concave front had already been in my mind, and I realized from the little figurines that we did not want a very deep cabinet. The showcase part had to be fairly shallow, so there would be no bad shadows in the corners; one would then see the figurines better. And the inward curve of the door should not be exaggerated; no need to be original or eccentric. We had arrived at a fairly comfortable height and size for the upper cabinet, the showcase part; I could make a realistic guess as to how the lower half should be.

I had some fine, dry pieces of cherry wood that I showed my

visitors. We agreed that, considering the figurines and the mood we wanted, this would be right. So I took my big old planks and cut rather thick sections for the sides, the principal parts of the upper and lower cabinet. A piece four inches thick would be enough for making the double-curved transition from the lower to the upper cabinet.

I had decided from the beginning that the curved members of the doors should be laminated. Partly because this is the strongest and most reliable construction, but also because it would make it easier for me to choose the grain to work with the curves. I laminated enough for

the upper and two lower doors plus two extra pieces, and, leaving these parts roughly sized, I planed the outsides of the side pieces to the shape I thought would go well with the inwardly curved front. Then, hopeful and eager, I set up the elements. My heart sank: There was something radically wrong. The lower cabinet was much narrower in appearance than I had presupposed. (I knew there would be a tendency to this because the sides of the cabinet are angled inward toward the front, and the lower part is deeper; but I did not realize that the effect would be so strong.) From the beginning, I thought I would bevel the top edge of each side to form a slight inward step where it meets the upper

cabinet. Now I saw this would not be enough to compensate for the "narrowness" below. In desperation more than anything else, I removed the frames of the lower door and put in two pieces of Lebanon cedar—two flat halves—just to give me a sense of how that part of the whole would appear if there were no framed doors with panels. And, indeed, it seemed wider. Strange, because in the frame-and-panel setup, I had the horizontal parts of the frame going all the way across; theoretically they *should* have helped to widen the cabinet. The whole idea of the frame and panel was a mistake. Well, that was a positive discovery. And yet, even with this variation of solid wood doors, something was wrong!

To make a long, chaotic story shorter: I needed to discover two things. First, that sweeping curved front piece sloping back and up had carried me away. *By itself,* as part of the lower cabinet, it was sweet; when I made a setup of the showcase part, with its door frame added to the curve, it was just too much—a pile-up. Second, the upper cabinet was too wide—by how much, I could not tell.

For a while these things were vague, only part of a deep disturbance as I stood, unhappy, looking. I think two days passed when I could not even look.

Then I took a deep breath, and jumped: I tore apart the lower cabinet with its finely curved piece, and sawed off almost two inches of both front curve and side pieces. I set up things again, pulled in the sides of the upper cabinet, reclamped the parts of the upper door. And, with this, I had reached a turning point.

Details remained, but there it was, a beginning I believed in. I could start working! Through the clouds, the sun shone. . . .

All of a sudden I had energy, I wanted to go on. There was the marvelous Lebanon cedar of which I made the doors, a joy to work with my planes. I could have done them in cherry wood, but the cherry I had was too straight lined. I felt, when I looked at my initial trial pieces, that what the lower part of the cabinet

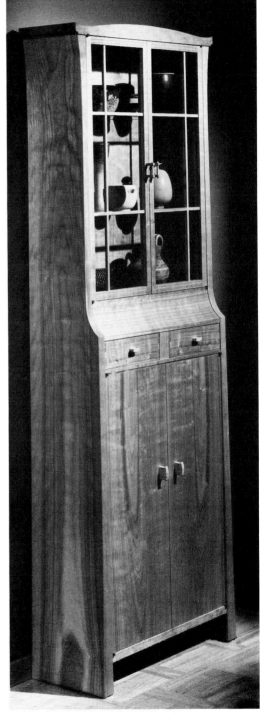

needed were doors with a ripple of some kind, a movement. Preferably there would be a slight upward slope. In other words, the lower parts of the doors, through the pattern of the wood, should appear wider than the upper part. This would help the optical experience of the cabinet.

As to the back piece for the showcase part: I wanted "live" wood there, too. With this came the guess that the shelves should be glass rather than wood.

I went on working. Some of the photos will, I think, give an idea of how things developed. This is a fairly complex piece, and, working as I do without drawings or absolute accuracy in various angles and shapes, there is, I suppose, a certain amount of asymmetry about the result. I hope that is not the same as inaccuracy or awkwardness, but is simply the absence of a rigid, "deep-freeze" look.

*Somewhere in the back of my mind were traces of this cabinet, also cherry wood, done in 1973, with its front curve so important to the piece. A shape balanced and quite pleasing in one instance, but misleading as a later influence.*

The door, with its five pieces of flat glass, has been fitted, the hinges located. Now, with everything ready, it has to be finally hung. I have the door part of the upper hinge atop the cabinet (the lower one is already fastened to the door), also two screws, a screwdriver . . . there's a stool to stand on. The completed door is fairly heavy; I must hold it vertical, firmly, unswaying, lift it—up and over—until I can coax the lower hinge onto its pin. Steady, no cramp or shakes now; "Hands, pick up the upper hinge half, slide it in place, pluck one screw, put it in, now the screwdriver, tighten, almost safe, almost. . . ."

There I am, up above the floor, the entire cabinet at stake, depending upon an understanding between a tired head—me—and my hands. Inwardly, sometimes audibly, I talk to them. Like Mermoz on those icy cliffs in the Andes (in St.-Exupery's *Wind, Sand and Stars*): "Hands, don't fail me now." The second screw is in, tight. Slowly, I close the door, open it, close it once more, as if to prove something. I step down from the stool. And, as someone who has been rescued from an icy ledge, I feel a happy fatigue envelop me.

We chose to have drawers inside the lower cabinet, and I made a "house" for these, a framework as the illustrations show. This served two purposes. First, it would be difficult to build in the proper frames or partitions for the drawers in the cabinet case itself; it was easier — and, I think, more sensible — to make a separate unit, which I then fitted into the cabinet tightly and fastened into place before I put in the back piece.

The drawer grips simply had to be the way they are because there was no space behind the doors for handles. We wanted the drawers as deep as possible for the sake of storage space, and I made these grips just on a guess, beginning with a small slot and then making inward cuts—inside and down, outside and up—toward the slot. Then I discovered I did not like the original straight slot I had made, so I carved

slight curves in its upper and lower edge. This changed the feel of the whole grip.

Another little thing happened, rather typical, one might say, of a person who works by feel rather than by certainty. The grips on the two right-hand drawers, which are somewhat larger than the left-hand drawers, turned out to be about one-eighth of an inch wider than the grips on the three smaller ones. This was not planned but rather discovered, right in the middle of the work. I did not realize from the beginning that the larger drawers should have slightly larger openings. It was during the task of fitting these, and looking at them, that I first began to see that, if all the grips were the same size, the ones on the two right-hand drawers would *appear* to be slightly smaller!

Looking back on this cabinet, I realize it is the closest I ever came to failing. Yet I did not *quite* fail. And I learned a great deal, although I paid a fairly high price for the learning. Actually, this piece, in an indirect way, got me to the state of exhaustion that finally put me in the hospital for a while. But that is another story.

# Some Favorite Tools

At a Stockholm museum of Asian art we had an exhibition of Japanese lacquer work. And in the very fine catalogue that accompanied the exhibit there was a description of the brushes so important to the marvelous decorative work done on such lacquered pieces.

The description began by saying that when one walked into the studio of a lacquer artist one could judge —by the brushes and the special polishing stones that are made for finishing the inside and the outside shapes of the lacquered pieces—the level of the artistry. About the brushes themselves: The very best were made from the hair of rats. Now mind you, not just any old rats, but rats that had lived on wooden ships. Because the ends of

the hairs of "modern" rats living in contaminated places are split, they are not suitable for these wonderful brushes.

I do not think it would be quite fair to say that any single tool is quite as important to a cabinetmaker as are brushes to a lacquer artist. Yet, for some of us, there are favorite tools, really precious ones. It is good to remind ourselves that the true value of a tool is not necessarily nostalgic or aesthetic; rather, the value rests in an awareness of the relationship of the person to the tool in the process for which the tool was intended to work. I think that some tools by their very nature achieve an intimate relationship with a certain person because he or she

really cares and learns to use them in a sensitive way. Then this mutual regard results in the person using the tools so well and with such enjoyment that they become an indelible part of the marks the craftsman leaves upon his work— the subtle details, lustrous surfaces, small carved edges, corners, and the like. So, what we are really talking about is a tool that can be made by a person or sometimes, though very rarely, bought, but that has in it something inseparable from that person and the relationship to his or her work. And if the relationship is total and simple and honest, then there will be evidence of this *mutual enjoyment,* as I would like to call it, the accord between the craftsman and his tools.

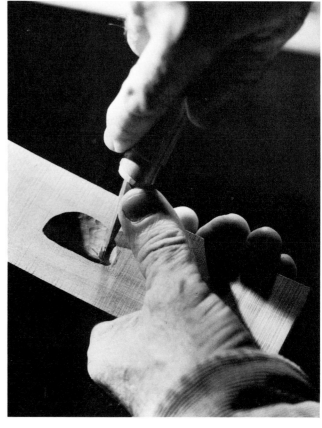

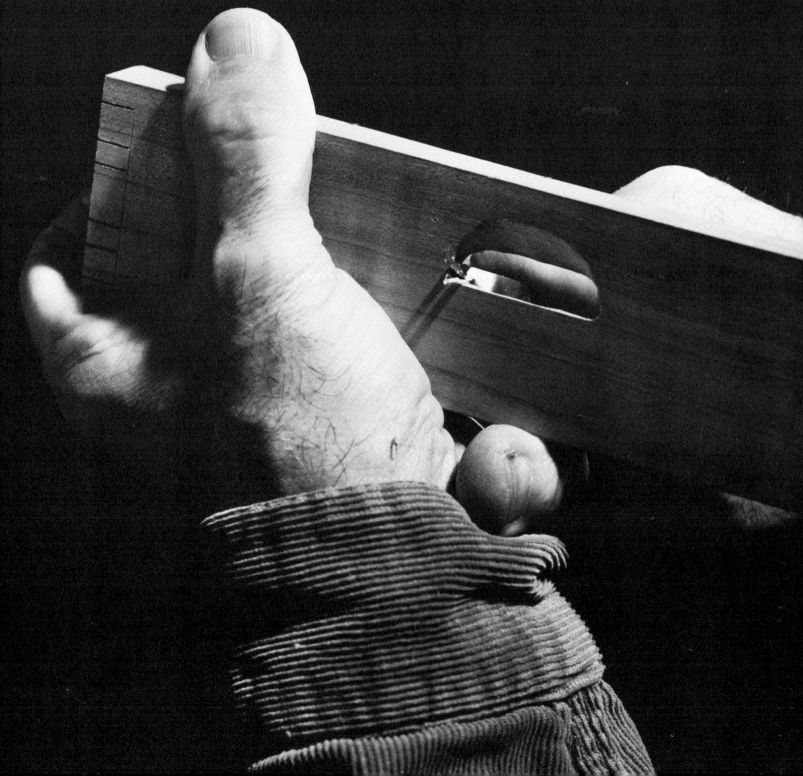

# Afterword

This fourth book by James Krenov may be thought of as an encore to his trilogy: *A Cabinetmaker's Notebook, The Fine Art of Cabinetmaking,* and *The Impractical Cabinetmaker.* It is not meant to signal a new broadside or to be his epitaph. Few North Americans (few outside of Scandinavia, for that matter) have had an opportunity to see Jim's cabinets themselves. Exhibitions are expensive to organize and they exist in a limited time frame at a fixed address. Since the first three books provoked the interest and spread his words, it seemed right to use a book again to share impressions of his pieces.

Jim's personal contacts while teaching two summer courses at Rochester Institute of Technology's School for American Craftsmen, during the organizing stages as well as the inaugural semester of Boston University's Program in Artisanry, and in many lectures and workshops (most notably, three summers with the Mendocino Woodworkers Association and Guild in Caspar, California, sponsored by the College of the Redwoods) have stirred a response from many woodworkers. Hundreds of letters from readers of his books confirm the interest in woodworking as (he writes) "A way of living rather than a way of making a living."

He is convinced (and convincing) of the value of the patient search; the joy of discovery; responsiveness to wood, tool, and intimate detail; and the self-satisfaction of developing and crafting each piece as fully as possible. Jim is primarily concerned with the *way* the work is being done—not the *how* of technique, but the *why* of attitude. The feelings, presence, and spirit of the maker are paramount.

He clarifies his position that a sense of caring is essential. A lingering search for the best wood, the best control, the best proportion, and the best relationship should be recognized as more important than lower price, faster delivery, or fresher design. Theatrical, striking, demanding, original objects place emphasis on the new that inevitably is dated, replaced, and eminently forgettable. It is not just the transience of the object that disturbs him; it is the futility of the activity and the competition it breeds. He laments that urgency is confused with, or substituted for, intensity, sensation replaces sensitivity, and recklessness supplants responsiveness.

Not all woodworkers are skilled, efficient, or inspired. They may understandably envy those who exceed them in productivity or originality. The insufficiency or infrequency of profit or prize depresses them as material or egocentric rewards elude them.

Krenov's words are balm for these

and others. He reassures them that ease and speed of accomplishment are but *one* measure of the worth of task and product. Emotional, spiritual, or ethical involvement is a personal attitude that increases the value of the activity, at least to the maker, and may also be recognizable as inherent in the object made with generosity and/or humility. His is not the only way, but it is a way worthy of consideration beside the many alternatives that are often thrust upon us.

There are typographic wood-workers, who manipulate, compli-cate, or ornament the alphabet with-out having a vocabulary or anything to say; the tract-writers, who in-voke, imprecate, or exhort; the graf-fiteers, who shock with smut or sar-casm; and the punsters, who slyly exaggerate or imitate another object. It's about time that we have a poet, a laureate whose cabinets are timeless compositions.

The pundits examine pinnacles and scan horizons. Their focus is too high or too distant for them to be aware of the understory in the forest of woodworkers. The carefully tended bonsai, miniature but resolute, is beneath their attention as are other gentle, restrained, and tentative varieties.

There *are* quiet, competent, gracious, articulate objects. The problem is that often exhibition coordinators and publishers are so used to one-upmanship dazzle and megawatt hype competing for media and public recognition that few have the nerve, discernment, or will left to honor simple beauty. Many disregarded people work in ways that fascinate and satisfy them but are ignored by the tastemakers. Krenov's way and words are welcomed by this multitude as verification of the worth of personal caring.

Jim's preference is for calm,

unpretentious objects that whisper lasting concern rather than demand quick attention. This book of his work serves, then, to illustrate pieces and their details that are too rarely displayed in North America.

Donald Lloyd McKinley
SHERIDAN COLLEGE OF APPLIED
ARTS AND TECHNOLOGY
MISSISSAUGA, ONTARIO

# Index

Born in Siberia, James Krenov spent his early years in Shanghai, China, and in Alaska, where his parents were teachers for the Bureau of Indian Affairs. He lived for some years in Seattle, Washington, attending school there and later building fine wooden boats for a number of years. In 1947 he left the United States to travel abroad and finally settled in Sweden. After studying furniture-making and design with Carl Malmsten in Stockholm, he set up his own workshop in Bromma (Stockholm) and began independent work as a cabinetmaker.

Krenov's work has been exhibited in several countries and is represented in the collections of museums in Sweden and abroad. He has lectured and given workshops in Sweden, Denmark, Canada, Austria, and England. In addition, he has travelled extensively in the United States, giving talks to fellow woodworkers and teaching at such geographically diverse places as the School for American Craftsmen at Rochester Institute of Technology, Boston University's Program in Artisanry (of which he was among the organizing spirits), and the Mendocino Woodworkers Association and Guild, under the auspices of the College of the Redwoods.